# Crime, Injustice and Christ

# Crime, Injustice and Christ

Timothy Chatmon

ISBN 1-59109-727-4

# Crime, Injustice and Christ

# CONTENTS

# ACKOWLEDGEMENTS

I will start but thanking my Lord and Savoir Jesus Christ for His Love, Grace and Mercy toward me, for without such I would not be here to share these few words with you.

I also want to thank my Love and Life my wife, without who's patience continuous encouragement and support has been a blessing to me while I have been going through the growing process to regain my footing in society after these last 5 ½ years of incarceration.

To my mother who has been a constant source of inspiration and motivation to the completion and this project. "Thanks"

Cece and Gwen sisters I love you, and to my church family and prison ministry see you soon.

Potters House thanks for the motivation to believe and conceive and achieve.

# "SPECIAL ADDITIONAL SECTION TO THE BOOK"

At the time of this writing there has been some very noteworthy occurrences take place in the world of crime and punishment.

The horrible crime in Central Park and the successful conviction of the 5 young African American youth goes to the very heart of this nations view on the relation of race as it relates to the enforcement Of criminal convictions based upon hysterics and false testimonies even by the defendants themselves.

The country learned a new vernacular "Wilding" and now the facts has come out that this entire event was a total fraud, It hit me exceptionally hard being where I have come from personally and have yet to entirely overcome.

There appears that no one has any care about the plight of the prisoners and that forms the scriptural base for this small add to the main body of the book.

'Also worth noting is the recent action by the ex Governor of Illinois George Ryan, whom recognized the frailty of the criminal justice system in the state of Illinois, and commuted the death sentences of over 170 death row prisoners, for the failure of the entirety of that system, and I believe speaks volumes of a even deeper more disturbing occurrence of wrongful conviction and mishandle of trials, and appellate procedures Nation wide, and leads to a total mistrust for those whom seek to take another's life so haphazardly, as it is here in my State of Texas where the executions take place so frequently that it no longer even get news attention.'

I believe that the Bible is replete with reference on the prison, and yet the people fail to acknowledge the significance of those behind bars, and seek to demonize them and forget the very bible that we read was in part written from behind prison bars.

From the Apostle Paul to The Prophet Jeremiah prison has been a constant reality to the body of Christ and his God.

This verse from The Psalms some up my feeling 142 v. 7

Bring my soul out of prison, that I may praise thy name.

The righteous shall compass me about; for thou shalt deal Bountifully with me.

Then I were reading in Ecclesiastes 4 v. 14

For out of prison he cometh to reign; Whereas also he that is born in his kingdom becometh poor.

Then I read again in the book of Isaiah 53 v. 8

He was taken from prison and from judgment;

And who shall declare his generation ?

For he was cut off out of the land of the living; for the transgression of my people was he stricken.

Then in another place I read as the Master called to account the Disciples in a place Peter said in the Gospel of Luke 22 v. 33

And he said unto him, Lord, I am ready to go with thee, both into prison, and to death.

Paul again spoke : Are they ministers of Christ?

(I speak as a fool) I am more; in labors more abundant, in stripes above measure, in prisons more frequently, in deaths often.

❧

1    Peter 3 v. 18-19 Says;

For Christ also hath once suffered for sins, the just for the unjust,

That he might bring us to God, being put to death in the flesh but made alive by the Spirit,

By whom also he went and preached unto the spirits in Prison.

Closing thoughts come from Psalms 79 v. 11

Let the sighing of the prisoner come before thee; according to the greatness of thy power preserve thou those that are appointed to die.

THIS IS MY PERSONAL FORWARD TO A WORK WHICH IS YET COMPLETE BUT QUOTING FROM 1 CORINTHIANS 2 VERSE 9 " EYE HATH NOT SEEN, NOR EAR HEARD, NEITHER

HAVE ENTERED INTO THE HEART OF MAN, THE THINGS WHICH GOD HATH PREPARED FOR THEM THAT LOVE HIM"

'SOMEONE ONCE SAID TO BEGIN A JOURNEY OF A THOUSAND MILES, YOU MUST START BY MAKING THE FIRST STEP'

So here, we begin this journey and foremost in my heart and spirit is to pause and give the utmost Praise and Thanks to my Lord and Savoir Jesus Christ!

For without, His unequivocal Love, Mercy, and Grace for me I would neither be alive, or able to bring forth these words to you.

Special thanks, And consideration has to be given to my mother Gloria, for the prayers and relentless support, I have received continuously threw my journey, and the Lord hearing the cry of the widow.

To my wife Dawn, for her support and love even when I did not deserve it and being a advent supporter threw the prison years.

Also sister Gwen, and Cecelia and the other family members who have given me their love and blessing over these years.

I have been a Bible searcher for 10 years, and one of the first scriptures I discovered and incorporated into my heart in the jail was.

Hebrews, 13 verse 23 " Know ye that our brother, Timothy, is set Free"

Know that I truly Love You All!

*This book is dedicated to all the brothers and sisters who are locked down doing hard time,and no one seem to be able to understand your plight. I feel you, and having served more than 17 years out of my life. If anyone knows I do.*
*I Love You Brother Timothy*

# PRELUDE: THE WILDERNESS YEARS.

I would like to begin this odyssey, by letting you know sincerely that you don't know the cost of the journey traveled to bring you this part of my story.

I believe, without a doubt my best spiritual quality is Faith,

Hebrews 11 verse 6 says;

But without Faith it is impossible to please him; for he that cometh to God must believe that he is, and that he is a rewarder of them that diligently seek him.

I preference this discourse by saying that I am a man of little formal education and present these conversations with you purely out of the passion and revelation that God alone has placed in me to share and hope to be a blessing to someone similarly situated and for those heading in the wrong direction, I say to you don't do it!

In order to bring this in the most truthful light, I will always attempt to be as transparent as possible, to accomplish what the Lord has placed on my heart to do.

Somewhere along the line, I must have made a conscious decision to enter into the underworld , and live 40 years in the wilderness.

I grew in a era of radicalism, and change in the United States with the militant's of the 1960's and 1970's and the Robin Hood mentality of rebellion that took hold because of the race wars and these rebellious spirits stayed with me over the course of these past 40 years herein the experience.

A little background on me would start of quite traditional in that I had a father and mother in the household whom worked very hard to provide for me and my two sisters.

We were poor by all standards living in a small town called Rockford,Il. On the west end of town but we did not think we were any different than anyone else in spite of the fact we had a outhouse and pump for water.

My father lacked any formal education and barely could read, and this were an obstacle to his ability to move up, because he had to help provide for his family during the period when the African American migration to the north from Mississippi.

Finally my dad found a job working for the sanitary district of Rockford.

This was a very nasty occupation in the sewer systems, and he worked hard and eventually was able to move us out of our old house into a new home back in 1970 and it felt so good to have my very own room.

I by no means speak about these things out of a sympathetic heart, But to set you up for the following story and how it is that I got there.

Let me start from the jump street and tell you I have been to nine penitentiaries in three states.

This is how it all began and my prayer in writing this, is that this could be a preventative measure for some other person, to avoid having to go through so great a cost to finally come to the truth that Jesus is the way the truth and the Life.

When I were a youth in school, I seem to be having problems dealing with a system that was not conducive to nurturing my educational needs.

Footnote: In 1989 the Rockford School District was cited for systematic racial discrimination in and against minorities and devised a formula for discrimination that rose to the level of a art form so Federal Court intervention lasted for about the last 13 years with massive building and restructuring of that system:

So is there any surprise now that I was having such trouble there in the sixth grade I decided to quit school and began hanging at the local chapter of the Black Panther Party Headquarters.

I learned more there about the struggle for the freedom of

the African People here and abroad than they ever could teach me in the school.

I helped serve free breakfast to the kids and went around to the locale merchants receiving the donations for the program.

Needless to say my parents were outraged and despised these activities severely, Back in those days they had what they used to call truant officers who would come out looking for kids like me and treat us like common criminals.

Looking back; these events marked my start in a life of crime, The truant officer convinced my parents to sign documents that declared me to be a delinquent and gave them the authority to place me in juvenile detention after a couple of violations.

Subsequently, I were sent off to the bad boys school called the Boys Farm of Durand, Il.

This was early in 1970, and thus was the beginning of a multitude of incarcerations and institutionalizations all starting from the truancy and lack of complete understanding of my parents to realize that signing those initial papers gave the state the right to place me in custody.

There were many of my contemporaries from the neighborhood there also, probably under similar circumstances.

We all bonded and formed our own little clique based upon the need to survive and gain strength in the abnormalities of our environment.

Seem that we started in earnest learning the tricks of the criminal trade right out the gate, There was at the time individual youth in there from 10 to 18 years of age.

By the time of my release 2 years later it was 1972, and my path had been charted for the next 25 years or so and the bitterness of heart and spirit had me bound to the street life.

Getting back home was like coming from a tour of duty, with the fresh game in my mouth and a quest to conquer the street, I hit the ground running.

Some of the older guys had started coming home from

the pen and hooked us up with the Disciple Street Gang from Chicago later called the Black Gangster Disciples.

So I started out being in the gang just because all my home boys were a part of this we learned the discipline of the code of the mob and Love, Life and Loyalty.

The concept seemed worthy at the time to be a betterment to our community and addressing some of the social situations with law enforcement so I were gong ho!

Later on the dope game came into play and destroyed the ethical concepts we had at the beginning and corrupted the entire nation.

Death before Dishonor.

The year of 1974 brought a series of tragic events to our family and to myself.

I was in the projects with my homeys and we had just acquired a stash of weapons and some one picked up a 357 magnum and pointed it at me and pulled the trigger, Seem like it happened in slow motion and I could almost see the bullet coming out of the gun and I made a slight turn and that saved my life because the bullet hit me in the right shoulder and not my neck and the doctor said that saved me.

I did not realize at the time the Hand of The Lord was watching over me.

Jeremiah: 1 verse 5 Says; Before I formed thee in the womb, I knew thee; and before thou camest forth out of the womb, I sanctified thee, And ordained thee a Prophet unto the nations.

By December of the same year a terrible event took place and as we all watched in horror my father burned to death in a house fire.

I believe this also had a profound effect on myself in that the experience marked for me a turn in events and view of the system at large, there was a situation that the city fire department would not respond to the fire even though they had a station only three short blocks away based in a city county rule and although we were almost in eye shot we were in the county and their department being all volunteers had to assemble and then respond and by that time it was too late.

This was one of my first experiences with the city of Rockford and the injustices therein;

Subconsciously I had become quite angry and probably started to delve into the world of drugs and alcohol seriously after that.

My older sister had already went off into the service at this time and was stationed in San Diego, Ca.

When she came home for the funeral of my father little did she know that I was already like Olivia, " lost and turned out."

I were fighting a case in the system for possession of marijuana and she came to court to testify that if they let me go I could come and live with her and go to school out in San Diego.

I never really had a formal church life although my mother and family were all members of Allen Chapel A.M.E.

Outside a couple of Sunday school lessons I seem far away from the Lord but he was never far away from me, By virtue of the prayers and intercession of my mother over the years and from her prayers for me the merciful hand of the Lord was always around with a hedge of protection on me in spite of myself.

Little did my sister know or realize that by the time she attempted to rescue her wayward brother, "I was a full fledged gangster."

The year was 1975 and San Diego, Ca. was a virtual paradise to me with the skill of the street that I had come to learn from back home I was hard core.

I started off in school for a couple of months, but this did not last long.

I quickly ran into some cats from my home town as well as some brothers coming out of the Vietnam conflict most of which like myself by this time were addicts and disenfranchised.

We had a little click that went out robbing and doing break ins to help supplement our ravenous appetite for the heroin and cocaine we had become addicted to.

Needless to say most of these guys were still active service in the various branches of the military and we seem to have a endless supply of drugs coming in daily of the ships from the naval bases.

Birds of a feather we all flocked together and soon started selling drugs to help offset our habits.

The drugs were fairly cheap and quite potent and me and my partner took overdoses on more than one occasion.

I were staying in a apartment complex with my sister and out of the entire complex my sister was the only one who actually had a job.

Once upon her arrival home from work she open the door to find me and a guy who later became my nephew's dad laying out with needles in our arms overdosed on drugs.

I know my sister was going crazy by this time and the final straw came for her a couple months later when one of my thug buddies girlfriend was cheated out of her pay at a dry cleaners in our area, He came and explain the situation to me and we decided to go and take matters into our own hands.

I grab my pistol and went to confront the guy and force the debt out of him and once he denied the payment, I decided to force payment.

I pulled my pistol and told the owner to relieve himself of everything.

The police were called and before we could make it back to our house we were caught and spent a little time in the County Jail.

Shortly after this incident my sister learned she had became pregnant, and knew she could no longer handle the lifestyle.

She decided that she was going back to Rockford, We caught a ride back home with two military guys we were acquainted with whom were heading to Chicago.

I went to a couple of my sources before we left and picked up me a supply of heroin, and about 10 pounds of that California weed to take along for the ride.

Once we arrived back home it was like I had never left and my guys were still on the block doing their thing.

I hit the ground running again, I quickly ran threw my

little stash and was up to about a couple hundred dollars a day in heroin.

I believe we were back from California a couple of months in the summer of 1976 and me and my cousin was hustling together and was caught in the process of robbing a service station and this would mark the start of my many long years in the Illinois Department of Corrections.

I were guilty and really did not want to waste the courts time with a trial, so I plead guilty to the charge and received a 4-8 year sentence.

I were only a 17 year old kid and arriving in the system back in those days were a real enlightening experience to say the least.

The options were minimal and the only facilities available unlike today they have a average of 29 facilities minimum, medium maximum and supermax, They only had the 4 maximum facilities from the days of the civil war. Statesville, Joliet, Pontiac, And Menard.

So these were the choices you had to chose from upon the classification at R&C.

I were pretty connected before I ever got to the joint because of my folks I grew up with and the gang affiliation yet I was still quite apprehensive about what lay ahead.

My very first day out of orientation as the fish line was walking down the long walk to the chow hall, there was a crew of my homies hollering out the broken windows of the cell house calling my name because they already knew I was coming.

Most of these same guys was they same ones, that I had been locked down with in the juvenile facilities back in 1970.

They had along with myself, had now graduated to the Big House!

"Now nothing I write in these pages in no way is to glorify these events, but to maybe bear witness to these truths and to maybe be a prevention to some of our youth and also to recognize the Love and Mercy of our Lord and Savoir Jesus Christ to save and restore even the most retched people that society has proclaimed to be cast away's."

The Bible says in the Gospel of Luke: 11 verse 33;

"No man, when he hath lighted a lamp, putteth it in a secret place, neither under a bushel, but on a lampstand,

That they who come in may see the light."

I am 17 years old and in the middle of Joliet State prison, the home of the likes of Al Capone and these other nefarious characters.

You have all heard the hard line that the strong shall survive and the weak shall parish.

I took this to heart, and were looking at the matters realistically and wanted to stand strong on what I believed in, my first day going to eat and standing in the line to get my tray a white guy serving in the meal line in what I could only see as a sign of deliberate aggression shoved a container of boiling hot coffee on me.

I am not a tough guy, and not looking to get in trouble , but in this type environment this act could not go unanswered.

The law of the jungle to effect and I sprang into action before I knew it and had leap across the counter like a wild tiger and hit the guy in the mouth and broke his jaw.

The guard tower in the chow hall, after realizing what had taken place pointed the gun down at me and they placed the cuffs on me and placed me in segregation.

I had yet to be processed into the system and not knowing which prison I would be sent to.

The word had got to one of the elder statesmen from my town of my situation and he had connections in the place and arranged for me to stay right there in Joliet

There was quite a few other cats from my town there also and we were just like old times.

The prison system was in the process of drastic changes back in the 1970's.

Racism was very prevalent in the 70's and you had various organizations of white supremacy operating with impunity and a large percentage of the staff members also.

The demographics had began to swing in the minority being the majority inside the walls.

Black and Hispanics now in significant numbers no longer would except the status quo of the violations of our human rights, and started to stand up for better program assignments and other benefits that the klan had control of.

They did not relinquish these things without a fight and the joint erupted in several riots.

After one riot took place I was singled out as a participant and taken to segregation once again this time they were determined not to let me back out into population and after about 60 days I was transferred over to Statesville Prison the year was 1977 and the scene there was not much different and the changes were taking place there also the staff in Statesville differed in that the blatant racist elements of the staff wore their colors and tattoo's openly.

Conditions were real harsh in Statesville and corruption was the order of the day, you could stay as high as you wanted on any type drugs or alcohol if you had the cash.

I believe there was approximately 5 thousand men in that facility at that time and I was pretty well known amongst my peers and had a measure of respect on the inside indoctrinated early on into the creed of the Gangster life and this was just another part of the Game.

I grew up fast in my new environment and started selling marijuana and hangin with my old buddies and new cats I had met threw the GD's.

I met the Chief Larry Hoover and many of the other infamous gangster of our time there in Statesville,

The staff was not to diverse and several race related murders took place against both sides.

Then there was a move to take the Chief out of the joint and he was moved to Pontiac in 1978 and a terrible riot took place wherein several guards were killed and hostages taken and after that it was a push to integrate the staff.

Big Jim Thompson, the then Governor of the State of Illinois at that time 1978 shortly after the riot flew into Statesville on the governors helicopter with a entourage of legislators and were in shock to see the tunnels of Statesville teaming with inmates running around like we were on the streets and they literally did have streets inside the most popular being State and Madison.

That day marked a historical event , in that would be the beginning of the great building process of the prison industrial complex of Illinois.

After leaving the prison that day Big Jim would issue orders to take back control of the joint and called for a immediate crackdown and there came storming in the cellhouses state police and troops of the guards shooting canisters of tear gas and violently beating anyone unfortunately caught outside their cell even the old men cleaning up the gallery.

They even went so far as to stack up body bags in the front of the Door to announce they where willing to kill everyone and had our names on them.

That came as a direct threat because of the loss of life the staff incurred in the Pontiac riots of 1978.

The administration believed that the orders came down from Statesville .

We continued on a indefinite lock down status for about six months and the living conditions were so bad that garbage and trash were stacked up knee deep and rats was running rampant.

The staff had refused to clean and the stench was so terrible that it was a health hazard.

So they eventually let us out of our cages, and like any animal that has been caged so long and treated with such severity almost immediately a guard was stabbed, and we went right back on another lock down .

I over the course of being in and out of Illinois prisons . I personally Witnessed the building of 25 prisons.

Now after the latest stabbing of the guard and the subsequent lock down and during the cell search, there was a open chute in the back of our cells that you can throw contraband out of your cell but the irony of this is they eventually had to stop somewhere and that just so happen to be in the back of my cell.

When the crew got to my cell and looked in the back chute there lay a half a dozen or more knives that me and my celly got charged for so we were hog tide and dragged off to segregation.

I really had been trying to stay clean at this time, because I had been scheduled to go before the Parole Board and this blew it for me and my celly, and this started a process before the Administrative Review Board.

I won my grievance and was released in late 1979 after serving the 4-8 year sentence.

I had literally grown up in the violent world of the penitentiary and now sent back out to my community without any formal education other than the criminal degree that I had earned on the inside.

I vowed in my mind not to ever return to the joint again and I never again robbed anything with a gun again but was a smarter criminal in my own mind.

The street was waiting to embrace the prodigal son with open arms.

I hit the street again with a renewed spirit, limited education and a criminal background.

Needless to say the Rockford, Il. Workforce was not very conducive to helping a ex- convict to re-integrate into society and I unwittingly had developed some powerful enemies in the Rockford Police Department.

I seem to be blackballed from the job market and after a failed attempt at going back to school , ( a certain police officer was in my class taking a social service course, started to harass me for my view and sought me out on the street .)

So I end up dropping the school and end up doing what I knew best and went back to the street full time.

I personally witness the first of the epidemic when crack cocaine hit the street first hand.

I began to use and sell drugs , and deal in the street life full time playing the so called player lifestyle with a couple of prostitutes on the side.

I were all things criminal , and my personal philosophy was

that if you are not physically hurting anyone you are not doing wrong.

I also began doing forgeries and credit card scams, this pre 1982 and was traveling across country just hustling and doing my thing.

I arrived back in Rockford around this time and one of my acquaintances from the hood I grew up with had heard about my hustle and he had his girlfriend with him, out of Wisconsin.

She had something like 5 kids and they basically beg me for some checks to cash , I looked at those kids in the car hungry and did try to help her and explain what to do for no repercussions, but as with most criminal endeavors she did not listen.

She was caught and made a deal with the State to get probation if she tell on the source of the paper.

She told the law it was a guy out of Rockford name T.C. and that was all they needed next thing I knew some of my people called me and said hey man we just seen you on crime stoppers.

I decided to leave Rockford and relocated to Dallas, Tx.

I came to Dallas and attempted to leave my past behind and got a job doing construction and going to school.

I completed courses in radio broadcasting at the Columbia School of Broadcasting.

I were offered many radio positions, and could not take them because I was wanted in Illinois.

So I decided to go back to Illinois and deal with the problem, so upon my return I was arrested and found out the situation was a little more serious than I imagined and the name that the law had in relation to those forgeries were wanted in 3 different States.

I was extradited from Illinois to Wisconsin to face trial and it came out that after the girl made her deal and got her freedom she was caught stealing at the mall and thus violated her probation and was sentenced to 9 years.

I started to research the law and found that because of this she would be unable to testify against me because of the impeachment law.

I had to pay about a thousand dollars and pleaded no contest to the charges and was free.

I went back to Rockford and attempted to get into the radio business but up to this day because of the barriers that exist in any urban music format in the minority community there it was a uphill battle.

I decided to start my own little production company and develop some of the locale talent, I rented a large building right in the heart of downtown Rockford.

Business was slow so to supplement my income I got a permit from the city to do promotional shows and parties.

I was doing a pretty good business and after a couple of months the police department approached me (crooked cops) and demanded that I pay them for allowing me to do business, I refused.

They began to start harassing me and my customers and coming in under the guise of the liquor commissioner looking for illegal sales, the people became fearful and stopped coming to the parties and I eventually had to close.

The crack cocaine had started to hit the street like wild fire and I have used a lot of drugs over the years but never got into the crack as far as using I always believe the devil himself manifested in crack.

I was no saint but had a certain code of ethics even on the street and saw many lives destroyed over the years behind crack and this was 1983 and many of those that started back then are still on crack walking zombies.

I got back in the drug business after this, and was working with a locale Jamaican kingpin who was handling a massive empire of sales and service.

He was having problems with the locale gang bangers sticking up his drug houses and I being life time member of the GDs had some insight and influence with many of those guys and brokered a deal with them to have a job.

This landed me a consultant position and advisor to the man and we had become quite close and my drugs came in unlimited supplies now and I were using about a thousand dollars a day.

The law could not break the operation so they set the Jamaican up and was able to deport him out of the country on a immigration case.

This was another instance of the law breaking the law to enforce the

Law.

There are to this day certain elements of the law enforcement community whom believe that if they consider you to be the bad guy thereby the end will justify any means.

My friend the Jamaican was gone now so my main connection was lost so I was just moving around and slanging a little here and there,

I ended up in Milwaukee, Wi. Hustling with one of my partners from Illinois and we had been up on the beach with a cat he had working packs in the town.

My partner did not have any license so I was driving his brand new canary yellow Cadillac Seville, and somewhere in Milwaukee the worker left a empty bottle on the floor of the car unbeknownst to us.

We were driving back to Illinois and when we entered Rockford a Illinois State Police under nothing other than racially profiling two black guys in a Cadillac.

Stopped the car and searched us based on the beer bottle in the back floor even though we tested negative for any alcohol , he found about a dime bag of marijuana in a case on the floor, also about 5 thousand dollars so he gave us a ultimatum one of us would have to go down for the weed and he will let the car and money stay.

It was something like a coin toss and I lost.

I fought the case for over 2 years and became weary and copped a plea for fine and probation and not long after that I violated my probation for refusing to play the game.

They give me 30 days in the county jail , and while there a friend that I had grew up with from the west side told me he had a cat that he wanted me to meet.

I did my time and got released and the guy called me and we met he was a white guy and he too was a consummate drug abuser in the third degree.

He was a shooter, smoker and tooter.

Seem like the guy had unlimited sources for cocaine and marijuana in Bales.

We started to do business together and I sold quantities to the brothers and he had a thing for black girls so I accommodated him in that also because I lived right on the stroll and knew quite a few prostitutes.

I began to wonder how this guy was able to maintain such a fierce habit and use so much of the product and not sell as much as he was using.

He seem to be fairly wealthy and had a 200 thousand dollar estate out in the country with several acres of land.

He had began to become increasingly paranoid , and confessed to me that people were after him and he had sank over 250 thousand in the rear with the drug debts.

I wondered whom he referred to and it was not long before I got the answer when a city police car pulled in my drive way and came up and knocked on my door asking for the guy.

The police was his supplier and the game had moved to another level that I personally was not comfortable with and I was looking for a exit strategy because I never like crooked cops and to become intimately involved in their operation was not my calling.

I had been a criminal for years but this was something I was unwilling to acquiesce to, and after maybe two weeks one of the front men for the organization a locale attorney come by my house to make me a proposal to take over the business and be successful in that working for them I would be protected.

I had a personal disdain for the law and was a true street criminal and could not see accepting such a proposition so I pulled my pistol out and ran the lawyer out of my neighborhood.

This act on my behalf just dug my already tenuous relation with the Rockford police department that much deeper.

I began to distance myself from the white guy that initiated this set of events, and went back to my old game plan of checks and credit cards.

This was the spring of 1989 and I was still out there hanging paper and doing alright far as my hustle was concerned.

I decided to go back out to my old west end neighborhood and see what my homies was up to and reminisce and kick war stories with the gangster's from the past.

(Footnote) "There is a serious lesson to be learned about going back."

Once I went out to the projects one of my prison associate's young nephew was in some trouble with some rival gang, and me and the uncle had been through some of the riots and other situations from my 1970's prison experience and we had a bond between us so it came quite natural to me to assist the nephew in the area of security and advisor.

I personally had love for the young brother, and had no compulsion about helping look out for the brother he was calling shots for the GDs out there and had a couple hundred soldiers in his camp.

His uncle was doing a bit up in Wisconsin and he had did some trouble shooting on my behalf so it was love .

There was a serious war going on at the time on the street and nephew was in it knee deep.

They made a living by extortion and shake downs of locale drug dealers and was quite successful in controlling some of the trade.

Many of those cats wanted him out of the way permanently and there was no shortage of others who shared that view.

During the summer of 1989 there was a war on the street and the guys were in a shoot out daily, I had explain the manner that the young brother should take in the way of security and he took it all with a grain of salt.

I personally did not profit one cent for this and did this out of Love,

There was a lot of drugs floating around and one summer night after all the daily rounds had been made, we were all gathered together in the projects about 10 guys drinking 'remy martin' and smoking weed.

At about 3 o'clock in the morning I decided I would call it a night, and I sent my girl over her mom's house to pick up my kids.

She returned and I talked a little more with nephew about some appointments we had the next day and he should go into his girls house and chill until later on, so me and a couple of his cousins walked nephew down to his door and we departed.

Now mind you nephew had several family members staying out there in the projects including sisters and grandma.

I assumed he was safe at that juncture, and went on to my house and went to sleep.

I got up and went over to the projects and knocked on nephew's door and his girl came out and said that he never came home last night, which was hard for me to believe because I personally saw him go in that morning.

I started to ask around to the guys and no one had seen or heard of Nephew since the time we had been out there chillin.

Some even reported that he had left town and I really could not believe it because of the fact we had several appointments scheduled and it did not seem logical and definitely out of character for him.

Maybe a month had passed and his mom put out a missing person report.

Within days of this the Illinois State Police received a call from a local farmer on the outskirts of Rockford that he had discovered a headless body out in one of his cornfields.

# Herein Begins My journey To Faith, Injustice & Redemption:

## I Called This Part II The Damascus Road Experience.

We have all heard this terminology before but I assure you it is the absolute truth in my testimony.

When the body of my guy was found do to the fact he were out in the county the agencies involved were numerous.

The jurisdiction of the State, County and City of Rockford Police with the primary being the County and State Police Special agents of the Department of Criminal Investigation.

The initial phase of their investigation was to locate those of us who allegedly had saw him last and this list encompassed dozens of friends, relatives and adversaries alike.

I along with several other individuals who had been in the projects the night we last seen nephew were taken into police headquarter for questioning .

I being quite confident that all the persons questioned told the truth as far as we all shared similar knowledge of the particular events as they related to the morning in the projects.

The fact also that me and my girl and 2 boys left together and several relatives of nephew could also bear witness to this.

Although my whereabouts surely was accounted for, again the Rockford Police Department Gang Crime Unit was enlisted to compile a suspect list for the State Police .

So is there any surprise that my name was at the top of the list.

Some overzealous Agents with the State Police seeking to short cut their investigation immediately when about a false theory that one of us had killed him.

They picked me up an additional 3 times, before they lied and came to my home under the pretext of me going to take a polygraph test .

( That they later admitted they never intended to give me.)

I was arrested September 29th 1989 for First Degree Murder, now during this time I never once attempted to flee or in any way not cooperate with the Police in the events that I had knowledge of .

I was in a state of shock and disbelief and assumed this to be some kind of terrible mistake and that my alibi would be checked and I would be Free.

Little did I know that at this time the deck was already stacked against any hope of me being released.

The Police had fabricated the testimony of a white prostitute to make the claim that she witness the crime and that the nephew was gun down in the middle of the projects in full view of his family and the body was left for a number of hours and then picked up by me and 2 brothers and dumped in the field.

I just knew in my heart this would not fly for the fact there was too many people that knew the truth.

I remained in a daze and quite numb and thought this only happens in the movies and to blacks in the 1950's.

In spite of my lifestyle and the other crimes I committed during my life I did not condone violence only as a means of self defense.

The authorities in this case clearly knew that I did not commit this crime of First Degree Murder.

They also informed me that 2 codefendants were being arrested simultaneously in Springfield, Il. And Minneapolis, Mn.

# The Road To Damascus

This is where my journey began through the maze of the 'Criminal Justice System'.

This also marks the road to where Jesus revealed himself to me!

The process had begin and I was to find out who these 2 codefendants were and some of the factual allegations that surrounded this mystery.

The only thing that we all shared in common is that we all Grew up together, So herein was the bases for the case, 'Guilt By Association' I believed in my heart at that time that all the guys would come forward and tell the truth and clear this up in the preliminary stages and I am still waiting. The position of the State was that this was a drug related execution.

The judge initially put the threat of the Death Penalty on the table as a possible option and I could hear the words but just was not digesting the scope of the situation for being in shock.

That night when I got back to my cell block despondent and paranoid about my life and everything going on,

I discovered a bible laying around on the floor somewhere and just picked it up and started to read it and I cannot recall anytime in my life that I read a bible and I settled in

The Book of Proverbs:

The first thing I can remember is the chapter 3 verse 5

"Trust in the Lord with all thine heart, and lean not unto thine own understanding.

In all thy ways acknowledge him, and he shall direct thy paths."

These passages just kept reverberating back and forth threw my mind and I began to claim and lay hold to these sayings.

Hebrews 11 v 1 says;

"Faith is the substance of things hoped for, the evidence of things not seen."

My measure of Faith allowed me to believe that God had set me up for these events to get my attention and to become a witness for him.

I began to pray that very night and on my knees praying, I begin to ask the Lord, why was these things happening to me, and I really cannot say if I were sleep in a dream or the vision was real.

I had this calming presence and feeling engulf my being and the Lord visited me at that very moment in time and the manifestation was of Jesus and he spoke clearly into my Spirit and said, ' Son do not worry about what is about to take place, because I am with you and will bring you out.'

Before I had been assigned a lawyer or anything the word of the Lord had already told me I would be coming out.

I had a strange sense of confidence henceforth and got on the phone the next day, and told my mother and family don't worry because I am coming home, I do not know when but I will be Free.

Things started to come out very fast in that the crux of the case against me was based entirely on the white prostitute who was the ex whore of one of my old childhood friend.

Threw the manipulation and deals made by the Prosecutor's Office, and the lead investigator and other police agents to Free her from a Oklahoma Prison and taking care of her pending charges in 3 other states and a grant of immunity, she agreed to testify against me.

The police gave her my name because of the fact she did not even know me.

I thought that this could not be happening in the State of Illinois 1989.

Rockford like other cities in America is notoriously racist

in the Administration of Justice when it comes to the rights of African Americans in the Court System.

The prevailing view at that time to the present, seem to be based primarily on a theory that if they present you as the Bad Guy then it is quite ok to Lie, Perjure and fabricate any or all the evidence to convict you, Now to the law I was the bad guy and admittedly have done some terrible things and have served time for the various crimes I committed.

Yet even I did not deserve to be persecuted for a crime that the authorities knew in advance I did not commit.

I had to believe that this was for a greater purpose and I had to walk it out to show God's Glory in my Life!

I had the very clear manifestation from the Lord and deep in my spirit I had no doubt, and that is easier to say than to walk out.

My mind still could not conceive how could they pull off a stunt like this.

I soon found out that it was as the days of old, were the combined malfeasance of the Police, Prosecutor's , The Judge,

Along with my 2 court appointed Public Defenders.

The only reason that I believe that I was prosecuted is the fact they had confidence in the proposition that they had in store for me and that I would take the deal.

They had set the stage to railroad all 3 of us and they attempted to have the divide and conquer technique to be employed to have someone to testify against the other 2.

I was called out of my cell and had a meeting with my 2 Defenders and a Prosecutor along with the Head of the Public Defenders Office. (He Is Now A Sitting Judge)

"Made me an offer They thought I could not Refuse"!

I had the opportunity to walk out the door that very day if I would cooperate and say that these others committed the crime and I just was a witness.

Needless to say I refused number 1 this would be a total lie and I said as much to them and their reply was unequivocally clear they did not care the question was did I want to go home?

I am no hero, but I also am not a liar and to have done something so terrible would have been unthinkable I was very pessimistic about the outcome after this but I trust in the revelation and vision that the Lord had gave me that I was coming out.

I realized at that moment, that the law knew that I was not guilty of this crime and that they wanted to use me.

My ' Pretenders' I mean Defenders told me point blank after that fateful day that they would not be able to defend me if I did not take the deal.

They made good on this during what can only be termed as a sham trial, now mind you this is pre O J Simpson and the opposite result and race card played to the utmost.

The deck was stacked with an all white jury, and the prosecutor did what can only be called racially motivated prejudice by saying to the all white jury that "He pointing to himself" "And Them pointing to the Jury" " Is not like Him pointing to me" I am from the projects on the West Side of town and unlike them would do anything"

END QUOTE.

I first off never lived in the projects but was there by choice and the race card did not end there.

The prosecution exploited this to the maximum in that we are dealing with a all white jury, and the witness being a white prostitute.

But the Bible says ; 1 Corinthians 1 verse 27:

God hath chosen the foolish things of the world to confound the wise;And God hath chosen the weak things of the world to confound the things which are mighty;

And base things of the world, and things which are despised,

Hath God chosen, Yea, and things which are not, to bring to nothing things that are,

That no flesh should glory in his presence.

I am the fool admittedly, and God has begin a work in me that he want to see complete.

Needless to say that after the trial begin and all the racial epithets used by the prosecution, to appeal to the passions and prejudices of the court and jury every conceivable act of misconduct had taken place from perjury of the Police and the only witness.

To every witness, who could bear witness to the truth summons were returned undeliverable by the Sheriff.

The deal was sealed when the judge sat sleeping on the bench, and the bailiff setting the daily newspaper in the jury room and after 8 days of trial and a different article appearing daily the jury took less than 2 hours to come back guilty.

I realized then as never before that the entire process was set up from the beginning and the Judge and everyone involved were fully complicit with these actions.

I had no choice at this time but to attempt to redress these issues and the Lord give me great revelations in the law and what steps had to be taken to preserve my rights.

The Public Defenders attempted to seal their malfeasance by filing a motion to have me sentenced without the benefit of proper Post trial relief in the form of appeal issues.

I literally had to have my mother go down to their office and make a physical threat because they refused to come see me by virtue of the fact of them selling me out.

So after a myriad of motions and Pro Se pleadings the Judge denied every issue to form the bases of a new trial.

I was sentenced to 35 years in the State Penitentiary Without Parole.

# 'Back to The Penitentiary The Year 1990'

I had accepted the Lord Jesus Christ before leaving the jail. In the Jail ministry bible study, with what has become a close associate of mine threw the years Pastor Byrd.

I arrived in Joliet once again in the summer of 1990, and extremely hot summer, and as if the Lord sent me a sign that I would be going threw the Storm!

There past right over the prison as we all were locked in our cell, hit Joliet with what now has been termed one of the most devastating tornados in the history of Joliet.

I was sent initially to Pontiac Prison and after about 3 months I made a transfer to Statesville Prison all three times maximum with the very worst that the state has incarcerated.

You recall that I was previously there 10 years earlier and it was like a old homecoming because most of the same guys who I had left there were still there 10 years later.

The only noticeable difference being that now the entire staff almost were minorities as well as the population.

I settled in for the routine of life behind the Walls;

If any of you have ever viewed a episode of OZ on H.B.O.

You get some of a idea of what the seen looked like.

I could never accept in my Spirit that I would be there for 35 years and retained a burning desire to be Free.

From day one I made a positive confession to all my distracter that I was not going to do all this time,

Now mind you every one in prison as the saying goes is not guilty of their crimes.

I were reluctant to even express to anyone my plight but found many others who like myself had been railroaded.

The only difference between many of them and me, I believed that the Lord would see me through just as he had promised.

This is a word to someone reading this book who have a promise from the Lord, whether you are Free Physically or in the bowels of the Beast stay Faithful and true to what the Lord has said.

This is very much a challenge for anyone and going back into the world of the penal system is shocking, With the rampant homosexuality and drugs used on a par with regular society.

This was all going on at the time of the now infamous Richard Speck tapes, that Bill Kurtis repeatedly showed on the A&E network.

I can personally bear witness that everything shown over those tapes were true, and that was just a shadow of the level of corruption.

I was still a member of the street organization and had become a bitter person in spite of the seed of hope burning down in my soul, and soon was back self medicating on alcohol and drugs to ease my pain and played the blame game, and begin to hate white people for what I perceived as their racism for my trial and went about warring against my past in the flesh and hoping and holding out in the Spirit for better things.

As the Apostle Paul wrote in the book of Romans; 7 verse 15:

"For that which I do I understand not; for what I would, that do I not; but what I hate, that do I.

I remained in anticipation and the chapel in Statesville although routinely used as a gathering place for the Gang Members to meet,

They also had some outstanding volunteers come in from Operation Push and blessed me to continue strong in the Lord, and to continue the struggle for justice and freedom.

I secured through the favor of the Lord a position coveted in prisons at the Law Library.

I had absolutely no working knowledge of the Law but

thanks be to God for looking beyond my ability and placing me in the right place.

They had literal geniuses in the Law including convicted Lawyers in there working that had helped untold persons regain their freedom or at the least get back to court for a fee.

I had limited resources and could not pay anyone for help, But God again showing himself in the mist of my situation, Had guys both Black and White give me tutorials and a basic concept of the Law.

Because they witnessed my personal dedication and determination to fight my case and learn the Law, They showed me how to marshal the facts of my case and to research and filing petitions.

The prison was so violent that we were constantly on lock down and that would delay the legal process,

I was housed in what they used to call West Beirut (B-House)

There was a lingering smell in the air of ' Death' and dimly lit like a dungeon of old.

There was a constant feeling of foreboding in that arena known as the Gladiator Dome.

The guards walked the cat walks with loaded shotguns and mini 14 assault rifles prepared to kill.

Most every inmate carried knives and all other types of weapons to commit mayhem.

All my direct appeals were denied by the Appellate and Supreme Court of the State of Illinois.

I again had a ineffective counsel on the appeal level in spite of the fact that I personally sent her numerous documents to include in my appeal she totally disregarded these.

I just kept petitioning the court Pro Se. at every opportunity and was constantly denied access.

I had again become quite angry and disenfranchised with anything related to the court, and eventually filed a Federal Habeas Corpus.

Eventually got a remand to the trial court for review.

God was still working on me and I did not realize the totality of the verse in 2 Corinthians 5 v 17;

Therefore, if any man be in Christ, he is a new creation;

Old things are passed away;

Behold, All things are become new.

# FORGIVENESS AND THE MIRACLE

I had over 5 years into the 35 year sentence without a release date in the century,
      With a 2008 parole date, I took another position in the B of I

Taking fingerprints and photo I D 's of the new arrivals and employees seeking jobs.

I also kept my position in the Law library part time, being locked up for a crime you did not commit is a strange burden to carry in itself, because first of even if you told anyone they would not believe you because of that old axiom.

I basically kept my business to myself and did not talk to anyone about my case except my homey and a couple of the staff at the B of I because I needed their permission to leave work early from time to time so I could go to the Law library to work on my case.

I will never forget that they would literally laugh in my face and tell me that I needed to let that mess go and do my time.

I just could not except this view point, and had simply stated to them all that I am going home.

I know I sounded like a fool to those doubters But God!

I went back to my cell-house after work and settled into my daily routine with a couple of my drinking buddies,

During this moment the Spirit of the Lord came upon me; and clearly said it was some issues that I needed to resolve around the hatred and bitterness I was harboring toward the prostitute in my case and she only attempted to save herself.

I will have to forgive her, and this is difficult. But the next one would be even more-so I will have to forgive the Police and the Prosecutor as well as the Judge and others who had testified and committed this wrongful act against me.

I was obedient to the 'Word of The Lord' and began to Pray for these individuals.

There was a Great weight lifted off of my shoulders and I had a better perspective about the Love of God than ever.

I really cannot say exactly when or how this had came about after but one-day as I was going about my business a convict from my hometown called me over to the phone and said, I have someone who wants to speak to you.

There he was, one of my co-defendants whom was acquitted of the same crime I was serving time for, and not coincidentally the white prostitutes pimp.

I had exhausted all of my State Court Appeals and had moved into the Federal District Court when this all took place and had just been appointed counsel who after the reading of my transcript did not believe a word I was telling him about my case.

The prostitute had confessed to a Catholic Father she had lied and perjured herself in this case and she was also willing to come forward and testify and to give a deposition.

The lawyer who had little faith initially now was a total God Send.

He took all the information that I had previously had rejected by every court in the State of Illinois, along with the deposition and other statements and presented these to the Federal Court and within a matter of 30 days the court issued a ruling that in essence said that if the State Court would not allow a Hearing to be held in this case they would.

This was the fall of 1994 and there is no second chance for proper preparation and we were totally prepared.

The Lord turned this matter around so fast after I was able to forgive the people behind my incarceration, that I had scarcely digested it all emotionally before I was sent from Statesville to the County Jail one day to presenting my case before the Judge to the granting of a Appeal bond. ***

# 'OUT OF PRISON BUT NOT YET FREE'

I was released but not yet free , Because the enemy had one more trick up his sleeve.

I were like a sheep led to the slaughter house and fell right into a trap.

They Appeal Bond assured one thing certain is that I would be available to the police to lay a trap, by virtue of the fact I could not leave their jurisdiction until the proceedings were over.

The first day I arrived home a investigator from the States Attorneys Office came by and knocked on my door as a forwarning of things to come.

This was the start of a cold calculated campaign of harassment by those very same police and officials who had initially set me up for the murder.

The word on the street was that the family of the victim that I were accused of killing was planning to exact revenge on me.

II Timothy 1 verse 7 says;
For God hath not given us the spirit of fear,
But of Power and Love, and of a sound mind.

I started of correct by sticking to the plan developed once I were free going to the church and fellowshipping with the Pastor I had known from bible study and doing odd jobs at my cousins garage.

Yet being exposed to my same old environment eventually started to wear me down with the constant threats and venom being spit my way, and I purposed in my own heart to defend myself and took my wife's pistol and armed myself. Forgetting the word and way I came to be Free in the first instant.

The Apostle James expressed; That we must count it all joy when ye fall into various trials,

Knowing this, that the testing of your faith worketh patience.

I had not fully matured spiritually to this point of my journey.

Then the inevitable took place the forces of the enemy caught me in a vulnerable stage and lured me to a particular location under the guise of a business deal.

I was selling used cars and had promised some of my old friends from the pen that I would do them a favor by making some runs around town and set up some financial arrangements and other help for them.

I met a acquaintance I had known for 20 years, and since the time I had been incarcerated he had become a police informant.

The informant told me he knew a guy who could help me sell the vehicles and sent me to his house,

Upon my arrival at the guys house I pulled next door to the place and before I could get out of the car and start a conversation with the guy a SWAT team jumped out of what they call a jump out van with automatic weapons drawn.

They immediately ran over and grab me and searched me and I did have a gun in my possession and this all was under the pretext of a drug raid and the irony being, I was the only one arrested.

They scarcely even went into the house the so called drug raid was allegedly stage for and I were taken to the offices of the Metro Narcotics Office.

The moment we walked into the door the very same Prosecutor from the murder case was standing there in the door with a sick smile on his face .

He personally staged part 2 of the saga and took narcotics

from a previous investigation and included them with me and contrived a charge of armed violence.

He also lied and stated to the media and the press that I had a stolen handgun from Kentucky.

This was in a attempt to cover for the malfeasance of the court and Judicial System in the murder case and to once again sway the public opinion to the view that I am the Bad Guy! I realized at once here we go again, and humbled myself and cried out to the Lord to forgive me for my not trusting in him totally to proclaim in the word I knowed to be true .

ISAIAH 54 verse 17: " No weapon that is formed against thee shall prosper, And every tongue that shall rise against thee in judgment thou shalt condemn."

I know exactly the corruption I would be facing, and that the formal rules of law did not apply.

I don't believe it was one official in the court house that did not know of me and my travails,

I went through all the usual motions and ran threw 3 court appointed attorneys and finally the Judge declared that we was going to trial in spite of the fact my lawyer said he could not defend me.

He said he had no defense for me and refused to go after the people who paid his salary and I once again were railroaded.

I had no illusions about the consequences of the court finding me guilty and tried to lock into the minimum sentence since the prosecutor insisted in my receiving another 25 years as revenge for my reversal of the prior murder conviction he said as much to one of the lawyers who got off my case early.

So after taking what is called a stipulated bench trial in order to preserve my right to Appeal, the Judge found me guilty of 3 counts of Armed Violence, Possession of Controlled Substance and Unlawful Possession of Weapons by a Felon.

I received the minimum sentence of 15 years. My only grace at this moment was in my Faith that the Lord had a reason to allow this to happen to me for his Glory.

There were also a issue of the purging of my spirit to rely on him and not myself.

I had to take serious inventory of my life and times and earnestly studied the word diligently with renewed passion.

I sought to see what it is the Lord would have me to do,

My friend the Pastor from the jail ministry never judge me or what I was going through and has really been a blessing to me over the years beginning in 1990.

This time around going back into the system I truly were a changed man and purposed in my spirit never again to allow the enemy to be able to trick or tempt me out of my God given position.

I had lost the entire decade of the 1990's before this journey came to a cruise and I say that because as of this writing I am still under the constraints of the D.O.C.

HEBREWS: 12 verse 2

I continued to; Look unto Jesus, as the author and finisher of my Faith.

I went back to the prison determined to sever all ties to the past and cut a cord with my past and started to go to the prison bible studies every week.

I prayed daily and continued in the Lord, and brought many brothers to church in the different prisons I have been to.

I got married in 1996 and to speak once again from the words of the Apostle Paul;

I count not myself to have apprehended; but this one thing I do, forgetting those things which are behind, and reaching forth unto those things which are before,

I press toward the mark for the prize of the high calling of God in Christ Jesus.

I once again lost all my appeals in the judicial system and needed nothing short of a miracle to get relief and so it was.

I were in my weekly bible study and it was a powerful anointing on the service there in Jacksonville Correctional Center, and the prison volunteer Elder Moore was speaking Prophetically and stood up and said point blank one of you are about to get a miracle and his time will be cut and he will be freed before his allotted time.

I claimed the word and constantly held fast to the word spoken in Faith.

I were sitting in my room one day watching T.B.N. and I saw the Bishop T.D. Jakes Preaching on a subject and I did not think much about him at the time but something had me to tune him in every Sunday which required me to sacrifice my meal because he came on at the very time the Sunday meal was being served.

Then he had a manpower conference that was televised through T.B.N. that year and I felt he really had a special heart for the prisoner and that one day I would attend his church.

Maybe in the course of a couple of months after this, God moved again through the system to set his son free.

The Illinois Supreme Court Struck down the law that I was sentenced under as unconstitutional and that required everyone to be re-sentenced and I were blessed once again to get my time cut just as the Prophecy had foretold.

I know that the forces could not except the turn of events once again, and I arranged this time not to play around in my town and had to relocate, and lo and behold my family had been living in Dallas since 1982 so this was the city for me to seek a new life and I am well on my way to restoration.

I have came to the Potters House and became a member about 1 year and am a member of the prison ministry.

I am writing these words so that maybe some of you experiencing a difficult set of circumstances and maybe even incarceration that you can overcome through Christ Jesus.

That you never give up or feel there is no way out.

The book of Romans Says: That if thou shalt confess with thy mouth the Lord Jesus,

And shalt believe in thine heart that God hath raised him from the dead, thou shalt be saved.

I have in conclusion found on this journey that Love covers a multitude of sin and when you hear these words harden not your heart but receive the word in all cheerfulness.

This is the testimony I leave with you at this point and it is still a challenge and the story is not over legally, or otherwise but once you make up in your mind that you are seeking change and make this known unto the Lord and develop the patience to persevere hardship as a good soldier the Lord is Faithful to complete the work he has started in Jesus Name!

Whenever man says no remember that we have a God that says Yes.

Let the Word be true and continue to Dream until the Dream manifest in your life I am too a Dreamer and although I have yet to reach the climax of the revelation that has been given me I wait patiently until the day of fruition.

I leave you with these passages of the scriptures to end this segment and until we talk again be Blessed and Encouraged.

The Third Epistle of John:

Beloved, I wish above all things that thou mayest prosper and be in health, even as thy soul prospereth.

I have many more things to say to you, and I am constantly Praying for all the ones that I left behind, and I Love You with the Love of Christ Jesus!

## GOD BLESS YOU BROTHERS AND SISTERS BROTHER TIMOTHY

# AUTOBIOGRAPHY

Timothy (T.C.) Chatmon , decided to write about his life after experiencing so many things in such a short period of time , and hope that in doing so can be a motivation and source of inspiration to the reader that is going through hardships and similar travails and being blessed to overcome.

Born June the 3rd 1959 in Rockford,Illlinois.

T.C. has lived most of his life in Rockord and also California and Texas.

After living in Rockford as a youth T.C. left school in the sixth grade and were subsequently was sent to the juvenile system and as a result has served multiple terms in nine different prisons and jails.

T.C. is self educated and learned to read while in prison, and eventually took his G.E.D and passed as the valedictorian of school district 428 and received certificates for outstanding academic achievement in the constitution and literature.

T.C. is now living in Texas and is a church member and in the ministry.

Henceforth the remainder of this BIO is contained on the other side.

I Pray this can be a blessing to the reader and to those thinking about turning to a life of crime DON'T!

Peace and Love